▲▲▲▲▲▲▲▲▲▲▲▲▲▲

CRAFTS
OF THE ANCIENT WORLD

THE CRAFTS AND CULTURE OF
THE VIKINGS

Joann Jovinelly and Jason Netelkos

the rosen publishing group's
rosen
central

To Joseph, the littlest Viking

Published in 2002 by The Rosen Publishing Group, Inc.
29 East 21st Street, New York, NY 10010

First Edition

Library of Congress Cataloging-in-Publication Data

Jovinelly, Joann.
The crafts and culture of the Vikings / Joann Jovinelly and Jason Netelkos.
p. cm. — (Crafts of the ancient world)
Includes bibliographical references (p.) and index.
ISBN 0-8239-3514-0
1. Vikings—Civilization. 2. Vikings—Material culture. [1. Vikings—Civilization.
2. Handicraft.]
I. Title. II. Series.
DL65 .J65 2001
948'.022—dc21

2001003889

Manufactured in the United States of America

Note to Parents
Some of these projects require tools or materials that can be dangerous if used improperly. Adult supervision will be necessary when projects require the use of a craft knife, an oven, a stovetop, plaster of paris, or pins and needles. Before starting any of the projects in this book, you may want to cover your work area with newspaper or plastic. In addition, we recommend using a piece of thick cardboard to protect surfaces while cutting with craft or mat knives. Parents, we encourage you to discuss safety with your children and note in advance which projects may require your supervision.

CONTENTS

More than 1,000 years ago (AD 800–1100), in a time known as the Viking Age, the area we now call Scandinavia was home to a civilization of people who were explorers, traders, and artisans.

The Vikings were extremely skilled ship-builders. They sailed across the Atlantic Ocean to Iceland, Greenland, and even as far as North America. They made these dangerous journeys in longboats—finely crafted wooden ships. According to archeologists and historians, the Vikings also traveled to France, England, and Russia. Although the exact reason for these expeditions is not known, it is believed that overpopulation, climate changes, or conflicts between leaders may have forced the Vikings to seek out new territory. For example, if a leader set laws that were too strict, his subjects may have wanted to begin a new settlement elsewhere.

Erik the Red

Aside from master-ful shipbuilding, the Vikings were legendary for attacking and raid-ing towns, monasteries, and churches all over Europe. In fact, "Viking" is an Old English word for pirate, which is how many Europeans thought of these often-violent people. Although many Vikings were quick to raid towns and kill people, the majority of Vikings were farmers or slaves who went about their daily work in an orderly and law-abiding fashion.

Through storytelling, some accounts of the Vikings' journeys were passed down from generation to genera-tion. Eventually, these stories—known as Viking sagas—were written down. One famous saga recounts how Greenland was settled by Eirik Torvoldsson, a famous Iceland-born Viking who is more commonly known as Erik the Red. Scientists, archeologists, and historians are able to learn about past civilizations

The map shows Viking routes across the Atlantic Ocean and Europe, including locations such as Greenland, Iceland, North America, Russia, and the Mediterranean Sea.

Viking Routes
- Earliest
- Erik the Red
- Leif Eriksson
- Ingvar
- Trading
- Ocean current

Historical names in parentheses

0 mi   600
0 km   600

NG MAPS
ART BY LASZLO KUBINYI

The Vikings were among the first people to travel the world, sailing to France, England, Russia, Iceland, and North America.

by studying the artifacts that people have left behind. Through such research, we have learned a great deal about what life must have been like for a man or woman who lived during the Viking Age.

DAILY LIFE

Everyday activities included scheduled time for working, farming, and trading with other Viking communities in the surrounding areas. Vikings also crafted items for personal use. They made many different things, such as woven cloth, elaborate silver and gold jewelry, leather shoes, and iron weapons. Daily living was difficult, but the heavy workload was shared among all the people.

Viking society was divided into groups, or classes. The highest class included the rich chieftains, or jarls. Often the jarls were Viking leaders who became rulers of their district. Jarls could sometimes become kings. Members of the largest class of Vikings were landowning farmers called karls. Others worked the land for landowners who were not farmers, while still others lived their lives as slaves. The slaves, who were called thralls, or *traells*, could sometimes buy their freedom in exchange for goods they had acquired or stolen. Most of the time, however, whole generations of families worked as slaves.

Bronze Age Viking village in Sweden

lived in longhouses, which were constructed from local materials. The houses had wooden or stone walls and thatched roofs made from straw and different types of grass. The hearth (fireplace) was located on one end of the longhouse, and it was here that the entire family would gather for warmth and their daily meals—of which there were two, one in the morning and one in the evening. During the early period of Viking civilization, families would do everything—sleep, eat, and socialize—in the one-room longhouse. It was not until later in the Viking era that longhouses were divided into rooms devoted to certain activities. For example, a longhouse may have had a spinning room, a weaving room, and a cooking room in addition to living quarters.

Laws were created in open-air meetings called things, which were twice-yearly assemblies of local leaders. A two-week meeting called an althing was held annually during the time of the summer solstice, the longest day of the year. At the althing, jarls would discuss major laws governing all Vikings. Disputes over land ownership and property theft were resolved as well. The althing also enabled the jarl community to take part in recreational activities such as wrestling, trading, and feasting.

Viking men and women often married and had large families, all of whom

In Viking communities, it was expected that you would be able to survive on your own once you were twelve years old. This meant that children learned skills from their parents. They were taught how to fish, hunt, cook, make clothing, and build shelters and

Opposite page: *Norsemen celebrated their discovery of the New World with a typical Viking meal, with drinks served in cow's horns. Vikings were often wrongly shown wearing horned or winged helmets.*

boats. Viking families lived in small communities that included farms, iron sheds (a place where iron tools were made), and barns in which cattle, pigs, and sheep were kept. In addition, some communities had a building in which coins were minted.

The Viking diet consisted of meat, fish, vegetables, and fruits. They preserved fish in salt (klippfish), and would store it for long periods. They hunted animals such as deer, duck, geese, and seals. The Vikings also knew which wild fruits and berries were safe to eat. Wheat and flax (a plant that can be spun into cloth) were commonly grown, as well as cabbage and onions. Vikings supplemented their meals with bread, cow's milk, and cheese. They were also skilled beer makers. Beer was usually served in a hollowed-out section of a cow's horn that was passed from person to person.

Odin, pictured here, was the Viking god of wisdom, language, and poetry.

RELIGION

The Vikings were pagans before they converted to Christianity late in the tenth century. Unlike Christians and Jews, who believe in the existence of one god, pagans believe in many gods. According to Viking legends, the gods peacefully resided in a heavenly fortress called Asgard. If a Viking warrior died in battle, it was believed that he ascended to Valhalla—a great hall within Asgard.

The Vikings believed in life after death. For this reason, they are often found buried in ships, along with possessions and food that they believed would be needed in the afterlife. Viking mythology also contains legends about what life would be like after the gods had been killed. Vikings believed that, at some future time, the final battle of the gods, Ragnarok, would be a match between good and evil forces. The Vikings were certain that some of the gods would survive this final battle and would go on to build new worlds.

Thor, the most popular god in the Viking religion, was the ruler of thunder and the sky. In honor of Thor, the althing (the summer meeting) always started on a Thursday, which was known then as "Thor's Day." Thor was so popular that his symbol—an image of the hammer he carried—was often carved on jewelry, boats, and furnishings. It was also common for families to tell stories based on the legends of Thor. One popular tale explained how he stole a large cauldron filled with beer from a group of giants so that the gods could have a party.

Another important Viking god was Odin, the god of war, wisdom, language, and poetry. Odin was also considered the god of kings, jarls, chieftains, and magicians. Viking legends say that Odin had two pet ravens, named Hugin and Munin, or "Thought" and "Memory." Odin was said to have set both free to fly around the world, eventually returning to him with all the knowledge they had gained.

Frey and his twin sister, Freyja, were the gods of love and fertility. When a couple wed, they would ask these gods to bless their partnership and grant them many children. Frey also ruled the Sun and the rain. Viking leaders would often ask Frey to ensure that their crops grew well. The Vikings worshiped other gods, too, but Thor, Odin, and Frey were among the most popular.

WARFARE

Much of what historians have learned about Viking warfare has come from written accounts of battles and voyages—the Viking sagas. When a Viking army leader, a thegn, needed to recruit others to join him in battle, he sent out a messenger who carried a large iron arrow through town. The arrow served as a signal to the townspeople, and the men who saw the arrow were supposed to join the army immediately. If a man refused to join, he could be outlawed and shunned from society. Outlaws could not fish,

trade, or join expeditions. Those who joined the thegn were called lids. It is believed that some of the other warriors were volunteer lids who fought for the treasure they stole, at times spending as many as thirty years away from their homes and families. These men were regarded as heroes.

Viking warriors often launched surprise attacks against their enemies. They used this strategy to compensate for the fact that their armies usually were smaller than those they were attacking, namely the English and continental Europeans. During the attacks, armed Vikings would stand together and form a makeshift wall. These land battles were called pitched battles, and there were also battles at sea. While the fighters on land were creating a wall of armed men, the seamen tied their longboats together into a kind of blockade that could not be broken by the enemy.

Researchers believe that it is because of their excellent navigational skills and shipbuilding techniques that Vikings were able to raid towns all over ancient Europe. The Europeans were horrified by the violent nature of the Vikings' surprise attacks. When raided, the majority of towns were powerless, and residents could do nothing but watch as their homes were invaded and

LANGUAGE

The Norse raider Rollo the Ranger attacks Paris.

Episodes from Viking sagas that were passed on from generation to generation were often woven into images on tapestries or carved into stone or wood. These sagas, or stories, usually illustrated famous battles or explained what daily life was like. The Vikings spoke in Old Norse, the same language from which modern Swedish, Norwegian, Icelandic, and Danish have developed. Since the Old Norse that was spoken throughout Scandinavia was similar from region to region, Vikings who were traveling or trading in nearby lands could communicate with each other easily. Aside from the woven or carved stories, most Viking tales were told orally through the act of storytelling. Fathers would spend evenings telling stories to their wives and children, while other storytellers or poets, called skalds, would entertain important leaders and jarls.

The Vikings used an alphabet called futhark that consisted of sixteen letters called runes. The word "rune" is derived from the Old Norse word "run," which meant mystery. The runes were drawn using only straight lines that were easy to carve. Since there was not a rune for every sound in the Old Norse language, writing was a rather limited method of communication. Vikings

their possessions stolen. As word of the terrible barbarians from the north spread throughout Europe, people tried, unsuccessfully, to prepare for their arrival.

The Vikings were so feared throughout Europe that they were commonly offered valuable objects in exchange for peace. This bribe was called danegeld, and it was given to Viking leaders who would then share it with their men.

carved runes into stone and wood wherever they traveled. Runes with the owner's name were often found on swords. Memorial stones were sometimes carved with runes that told the tale of how warriors were killed. It was generally believed that the runes held magical powers. For instance, if a sword was carved with a name or an inscription, that weapon was thought to hold special, supernatural properties. Runes first appeared around AD 200 and, at that time, there were twenty-four characters. By AD 800, the Vikings had paired down the runes to sixteen characters. By the end of the twelfth century, the Viking sagas were written on calfskin, which was used as a kind of paper. These stories were not written in runes, but in Latin, the language of Christian missionaries, and were translated and copied by hand through the ages. Future generations would read the sagas rather than hear them recited.

ART

The Vikings were well-known artisans and were recognized for the beautiful objects and crafts that they made. In addition to iron objects such as tools and arrowheads, the Vikings made stunning silver and gold jewelry, fine leather shoes and helmets, intricate games and game pieces, and sculptures of various sizes. Craftspeople worked with natural materials such as amber, animal bones, and metals, including pewter and bronze.

Viking women were responsible for assembling their families' clothing. They created complicated fabric trims and borders for each family member's clothing, and dyed fabrics bright colors from natural pigments. (For example, red came from the boiled skin of red onions.) Some of this clothing was very fancy, featuring extremely complex patterns. According to archeologists, most Vikings wore a variety of different fabrics such as wool, linen, and imported silk. Sometimes these fabrics were trimmed in animal fur and leather.

In the later period of the Viking age, it was common for a town to have separate workshops for its best artisans. Everything from glass jewelry to leather boots was made in its divided quarters. Artisans fashioned blades for ice skates and hair combs from animal bones; carpenters carved spoons and bowls, furnishings, and boats. Nearby, potters, tanners (craftsmen who work with leather), and sculptors crafted their wares. Although they were known for their savagery in war, the Vikings must also be remembered for their sophisticated artistry.

Navigation and Shipbuilding

The typical strategy of Viking warriors was to sail briskly along a foreign shoreline and invade nearby towns and villages. As their navigational skills sharpened, they sailed across broader areas, conquering new lands along the way. The Vikings were skilled navigators, though they had none of the instruments that mariners use today. Viking sailors relied mostly upon the sun and the stars to guide them. They also searched for other recognizable signs—such as wave patterns and the presence of certain kinds of sea animals—to help them estimate their location.

Although the Vikings developed several different kinds of ships, their most famous boat was the longboat, a type of warship. Longboats were shallow, canoelike vessels that could sail swiftly through rough seas. Warriors were able to carry their longboats and repair them if necessary. Each ship had a woolen sail that was often striped red, blue, and white. Each longboat was capable of holding up to fifty men, forming a team of rowers. One longboat that was discovered in Denmark is

This replica of a Viking longboat is fully functional and has a colorful sail. The Vikings often used blood-red dyes on sails to strike fear into the hearts of their enemies.

ninety feet long. Archeologists believe that this boat was filled with stones and purposefully sunk during a battle around the year AD 1000.

The majority of the longboats were crafted from oak and were made up of several parts, each serving a different purpose. The most important part was called a keel. This section formed the solid oak backbone of the ship and helped it sail in a straight line. The remaining sections of the longboat were called its rib and mast. The rib extended from the keel and created the boat's skeleton, or its structure. The mast is the long pole extending upward from the longboat's center and upon which the sail was hung.

After the main parts were assembled, the sides of the longboat were formed from long planks of overlapping wood. The planks were nailed together with wooden pegs and the spaces between the planks were then stuffed with straw, sand, hair, and mud to keep the boat watertight.

Because the Vikings were so feared, their longboats were associated with raiding and warfare. The ships were often called serpents of the sea because they were crowned with snakelike figureheads on the front (prow) and rear (stern) sections, making them look even more terrifying.

A replica of a longboat's figurehead. The snakelike shape and curved images of serpents made these boats, often called serpents of the sea, seem fearsome to the victims of the Vikings.

One of the only surviving Viking longboats, this ship is exhibited at the Viking Museum in Norway.

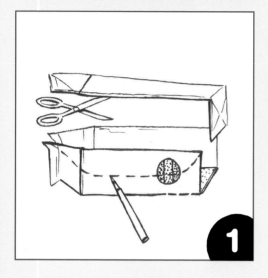

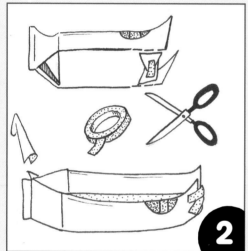

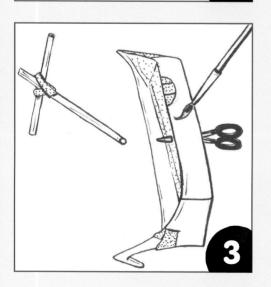

Viking Longboat

Build a model of a ship found in 1880 by archeologists in Gokstad, Norway.

YOU WILL NEED
- Quart-sized carton
- Masking tape
- Scissors
- Felt-tip pen
- White glue
- Drinking straws
- Paper grocery bag
- String
- Craft paint
- Toothpick

Step 1
Insert scissors through the open spout of an empty quart-sized carton. Cut straight lines along the edges of its back panel and through to its bottom square, as shown. With a felt-tip pen, draw an outline of your boat on both side panels, and cut along those drawn lines.

Step 2
Cut two three-inch slits along the edges of the carton (the side opposite the spout). Fold the cut edges together and secure with tape. Next, tape the exterior sides together in the same manner. You may also add some detail, such as taping a cone shape to one end, creating a figurehead.

Step 3
Tape two drinking straws together to form a cross. This will be the longboat's mast. Carefully puncture a hole in the center of the longboat's floor using the tip of your scissors. To simulate a wooden surface on its exterior, apply layers of masking tape in strips before painting the boat and mast brown.

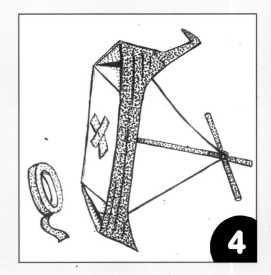

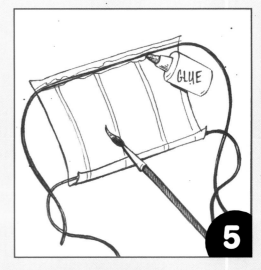

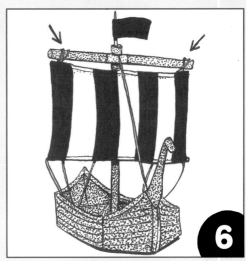

Step 4

Insert the mast through the hole and tape it on the reverse side. Tie a long string around the top of the mast and attach the ends to the front and back of the interior of the boat with tape. This will help keep the mast standing straight, so tape the strings tautly.

Step 5

Cut a rectangle from a brown paper grocery bag, approximately the same size as the width of the mast. This will be your longboat's sail. Paint designs on it such as stripes and set aside to dry. Glue long pieces of string along its top and bottom edges. Allow them to extend several inches beyond each corner.

Step 6

With the excess string, tie the sail to the top of the mast. Add a flag by gluing a paper rectangle to a toothpick, and then glue it to the mast top.

Weapons and Warfare I

According to the sagas, Viking raids began around AD 800. Most were carried out by small parties of men who traveled by foot or by sea in longboats. At first, the Viking warriors raided only wealthy churches and monasteries because monks offered little resistance, and the riches found there were abundant. Later, the Vikings turned their attention toward towns and villages throughout Europe, stealing even more land, valuables, and slaves.

Historians know that the Vikings began raiding from the North Sea and the English Channel. Later, they ventured farther inland, sailing their longboats through European rivers such as the Rhine and the Seine. Most of England, Ireland, and Scotland were seized during different raids, as was Paris, France. The Vikings also sailed across the Baltic Sea into Russia and then into the lands of Islam (an area that encompassed modern-day Saudi Arabia, Turkey, Syria, and Egypt). One of the earliest Viking raids, in AD 793,

Actors reenact a Viking battle using replicas of helmets, shields, swords, axes, and spears.

took place at the monastery at Lindisfarne, located on the northern coast of England. The invasion was written about in the famous text, the *Anglo-Saxon Chronicle*, which states: "The Vikings trampled the holy places with their dirty feet, dug up the altars, and seized all the treasures of the holy church. They killed some of the brothers. Some they took away with them in chains. Many they drove out, naked and loaded with insults, and some they drowned in the sea."

The most famous and brutal of the Viking warriors were called berserkers. They were known for their fierce fighting methods and for their belief that they could not be wounded. During pitched battles, berserkers became so agitated that they often ground their teeth together or chewed on their shields. Some historians also think that the berserkers believed that a mushroom called fly agaric would give them magical powers. Fly agaric is known to inspire rage (and therefore make a person more physically aggressive).

The term "berserker" may have originated from the bearskin cloaks (berserks) that were often worn by warriors. Preparation for battle was referred to as "going berserk." When the fighting began, the team of warriors fired arrows. Then, the spears followed. Whoever remained then fought using hand-to-hand combat.

Viking warriors thought the fly agaric mushroom gave them magical protection against injuries.

This iron spearhead decorated with silver was used as a thrusting weapon in battles.

This Viking helmet—the only complete one ever found—was discovered in Gjermundbu, Norway.

Viking Helmet

Dress like a Viking by wearing a helmet similar to those worn by ancient warriors.

YOU WILL NEED
- White glue
- Water
- Brush
- Large balloon
- Recycled newspaper
- Scissors
- Hole puncher
- Cardboard scraps
- Paper fasteners
- Craft paint
- Pushpins

Step 1

Make a papier-mâché paste by mixing together a solution of white glue and water. (Mix three parts glue to one part water.)

Step 2

Cover more than half of an inflated balloon with the newspaper strips dipped into the glue solution, as shown. Make the layers even. Allow it to dry overnight.

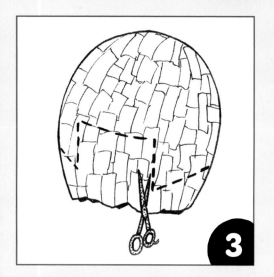

Step 3

When the surface has hardened, pop and remove the balloon. Trim any rough patches with scissors. Cut a rectangle at the front of your helmet. This cut is where the nose guard will be placed.

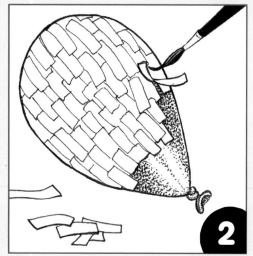

Step 4

Cut two long strips of cardboard (the sides of a pizza box work well) to run along the length and width of the helmet, as shown. Bend the cardboard by first rolling it around a pencil. Punch holes along the strips at regular intervals. Glue the two bands to the helmet as shown. Force a push pin through the bands' holes

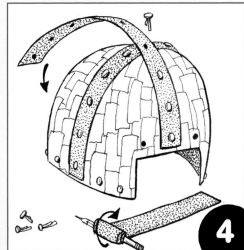

until the pin pierces the helmet. Place paper fasteners in these holes and fold back the ends so that they are flush with the inside of the helmet.

Step 5

Cut a piece of cardboard to make a nose guard for your helmet. A simple T shape will do, or make goggles. Puncture three holes along its top. Then glue the guard to the helmet. Force the pushpins through the holes until you pierce the helmet. Place paper fasteners in these holes and fold back their ends.

Step 6

Paint the helmet using metallic silver paint. When it dries, rub a small amount of black paint on the helmet surface to give it a "battle scarred" look.

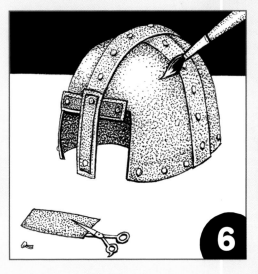

Weapons and Warfare II

Most Viking weapons were made of metals, except for shields, which were constructed of wooden planks. The rounded center of the shield, called a boss, was made of iron. The boss was designed to protect the warrior's hand during battle. A warrior's spear, ax, shield, and helmet were his most important personal possessions. They were usually crafted from layers of iron. Sometimes the sword handles were beautifully decorated with complex designs made of silver or copper.

A warrior's most important weapon was his ax. Occasionally, an ax was given a special name to celebrate its importance, such as Fierce, Leg-biter, or Adder. Before the arrival of Christianity, warriors were buried with their shields and spears. Warriors believed that they would need their weapons in Valhalla, the final home for dead Viking warriors. Other times, these items were handed down from father to son.

Iron ax blades, the most important weapons in a Viking's arsenal, were often inlaid with silver in beautiful patterns.

Viking helmets fit closely to the head and were made of leather or iron. Most helmets had nose guards that were lightly decorated, but never with horns or wings as they are sometimes depicted. Viking warriors had to provide their own arms, or weapons. There was no specific type of uniform or shield that they were supposed to wear or hold. Although certain styles of weaponry were common, every man outfitted himself for battle.

Only wealthy Vikings could afford a coat of armor, a heavy shirt made of iron. Made of thousands of small, hand-crafted metal rings, the chain-mail shirt was also called a *byrnie* and was carried to battles on long sticks. When warriors couldn't afford a chain-mail shirt, they dressed in plain leather instead. Although it didn't offer much protection, leather was more effective than a simple oversized tunic—the other option for warriors without the chain-mail shirt.

Odin was the Viking god of war. When a Viking died in battle, warriors would retrieve his body so he could be burned in a funeral pyre. According to Viking legends, if a dead warrior was burned in this way, his spirit would go to Valhalla. Other Vikings were buried in their longboats with their most valued possessions. Sometimes dogs, horses, and even slaves would be buried with them. If a Viking did not own a boat, his or her body would be buried underground, and stones in the shape of a boat would be placed to mark his or her gravesite.

Viking swords were often double-edged. Their hilts were usually decorated with silver or brass.

Actors pose behind their shields while reenacting a Viking battle in Denmark.

Viking Shield

Reenact a battle using authentic-looking shields.

YOU WILL NEED
- Recycled pizza box
- 9 plastic bottle caps
- Scissors
- Pencil
- Thumbtacks
- Paper bowl
- White glue
- Masking tape
- Craft paint

Step 1
Draw a large circle spanning an entire surface of a pizza box lid. Cut the circle from the box with scissors.

Step 2
Use this cut circle to trace another circle on the bottom of the box. Cut this one out as well.

Step 3
Cut two slits at the center of one of the circles, as shown. Use one side of the pizza box as a handle and slip it through the slits. Fold the ends and tape it securely on the opposite side.

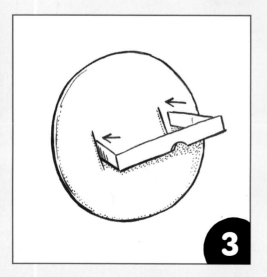

Step 4
On the surface of the other circle, arrange the nine bottle caps, placing one cap in the center; set the other caps around the outer rim of the circle, leaving a 1/2-inch border. Glue these bottle caps to the cardboard circle at regular intervals.

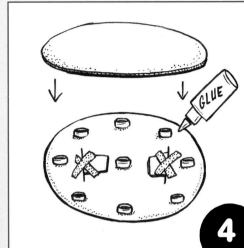

4

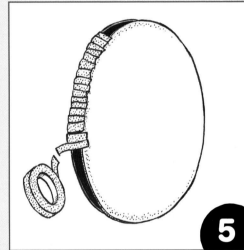

5

Step 5
Set the other cardboard circle onto the caps so both circles are aligned. Tape the two circle sides together with strips of masking tape, as shown.

Step 6
Paint the front surface of the shield in a swirl or cross design. Glue a paper bowl to the center and glue silver thumbtacks along the edges.

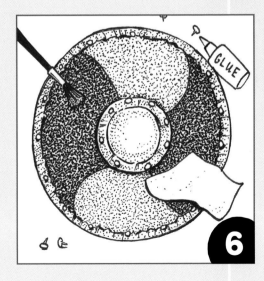

6

Travel and Trade I

The Vikings often sought out new land in order to settle it, but they simply wanted to raid other towns in order to obtain more riches. Most of the Viking explorers came from Norge (present-day Norway), where they learned to sail their longboats in the Atlantic Ocean. This is how they discovered Iceland, Greenland, and North America, which was then called Vinland.

The Vikings brought many goods—wood, raw iron, animal skins and furs, amber, and animal bones that were good for carving—with them on their journeys because they often traded with foreigners. Based on the variety of objects of foreign design that were buried with wealthy Viking warriors and kings, historians believe that the Vikings had firmly established trade routes. The runic inscriptions that have been found all over the world further illustrate how far and how frequently the Vikings traveled.

Since there was no common currency, or money, in Viking society, goods were commonly traded for other

On their journeys, the Vikings brought with them many goods, such as iron, furs, metals, coins, and bones, for trading with foreigners.

goods. Today, this process is called bartering. From bartering, the Viking explorers obtained many useful things such as wheat, salt, pottery, glass, precious metals like silver and gold, spices, and silk cloth. When attempting a trade of equal value, the Vikings used a scale and assorted weights. These palm-sized scales have been found in many Viking settlements.

The scales consisted of two bronze bowls of equal size and weight that were attached to two copper wires hung from a length of metal tubing. Due to the simple, compact design of the scales, traders could fold them into a special box or pouch. When items were weighed for trading, they were placed in one bowl while other objects or measured weights were placed in the other bowl. These small iron weights were normally carried in sets of five. Each one represented a different weight that was sometimes inscribed on the iron. If a trader did not have weights, he may have traded with raw bits of silver or gold that could also be measured on the scale.

Much later, around AD 1000–1100, some Viking towns became known as trading centers where sailors would travel to trade goods. There were well-known marketplaces in Sweden (Birka), Norway (Kaupang), and Denmark (Hedeby). Merchants sailed from France, Russia, Spain, and even the Middle East, in order to trade goods such as Arabian silver, Byzantine silks, and Russian and German glass.

Late in the Viking era, glass was imported from Russia and Germany.

Vikings used scales to weigh items they were trading in order to ensure a fair exchange.

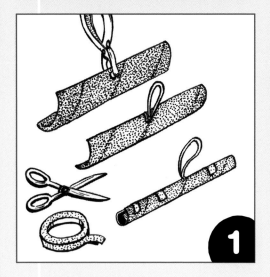

Trading Scale

Using a scale, reenact trading that took place in the market-place of Birka, a busy center for Viking artisans in AD *850.*

YOU WILL NEED
- Cardboard paper-towel roll
- Golden-colored paper clips
- Salt clay (see recipe on page 34)
- String
- Hole puncher
- 2 paper bowls
- Craft paint
- Masking tape

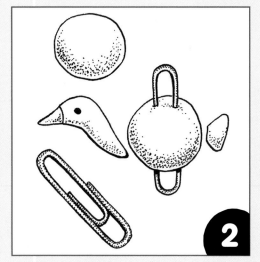

Step 1
Cut a paper-towel roll down the middle. Punch a hole at the center of the long edge, as shown. Thread a piece of string through this hole and knot it with a loop. Roll the tube into a tighter, slender roll. Tape securely.

Step 2
Make two clay beads using the salt clay recipe on page 34. Insert a paper clip through each bead. You could add details to them with small pieces of clay, as shown.

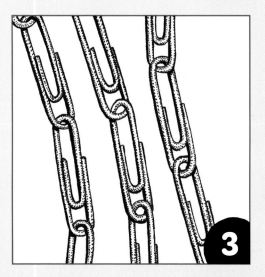

Step 3
For the chains of the scale, string six strands of paper clips. Make each strand ten paper clips long. Then, make two more paper clip chains using only four clips each. Insert the four clip chains at each open end of your cardboard tube and tape them in place.

Step 4
Join the dangling end of each short paper clip chain to the top of a clay bead. Attach three long paper clip chains to the bottom of each clay bead.

Step 5
Mark each paper bowl along the rim, as if it were a clockface. Punch holes marking two o'clock, seven o'clock, and ten o'clock.

Step 6
Attach the bottom of the long chains to the bowls and tape them securely in place. Your scale is now constructed. Paint it with gold and black craft paint for an authentic appearance.

Travel and Trade II

Eventually, Viking society moved away from bartering for goods and toward the use of currency. This made trading much simpler since goods could be paid for with coins instead of people having to go to the trouble of using scales to determine the equal weight of each item. Usually, the coins were crafted from silver, a soft metal that is easy to inscribe. They often featured portraits of kings or illustrations of ships and runes. Though the first Danish coins date from the ninth century, the widespread use of currency did not occur until the reign of King Harald Bluetooth in AD 975.

First, a die would be cast that would become the mold used to create a series of identical coins. The die would be inscribed with a certain design and then that design would be tested on a strip of lead. If the mold was considered satisfactory, the coins would be minted, or made in mass quantities. The coins themselves were crudely designed, often varying in size and weight, but they served to increase trade within the community and along Viking trade routes to known markets.

The earliest Vikings exchanged foreign coins, such as those from Arabia (an area encompassing modern-day Saudia Arabia, Syria, and Iraq), by their individual weight, not according to their value. They also kept many broken coin pieces on hand to

Below is an example of futhark, the Viking alphabet. Each letter corresponds with the letter of the English alphabet above it.

F	U	Th	A	R	K	H	N	I	A	S	T	B	M	L	R

use as weights. When a trader offered an item for sale—a piece of amber, for example—the buyer would hand over enough coins to match the weight of the object. If the comparison remained uneven, the trader would add pieces of broken coins to the scale until the weight of the coins equaled the weight of the amber.

This game piece, carved from amber, was found in Roholte, Denmark.

In the tenth century, trading centers such as Birka—now Stockholm, Sweden—were bustling with activity. Birka was protected by a wooden and dirt-filled wall, and had a population of several thousand people who protected and served the city's visitors. Local Vikings, as well as foreign visitors traveling along established trading routes, sailed to Birka to buy and sell their goods. In these market centers, both food and goods were plentiful. Regardless of the overcrowded streets, the local population was lawful. People of every ethnicity, speaking as many as a dozen different languages, shared one common goal—commerce.

The widespread use of Viking currency is attested to by the fact that some Viking coins were still accepted as payment some 150 years after the civilization itself had waned.

These Viking coins were found at the ancient Viking marketplace in Birka, Sweden.

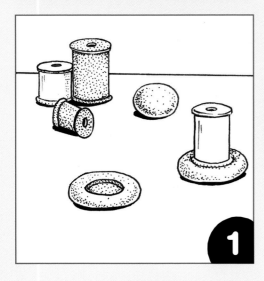

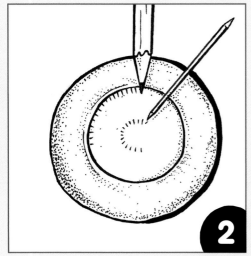

Viking Coins

Amass your own treasure trove of coins like those ordered by Viking king Harald Bluetooth in AD *975.*

YOU WILL NEED
- Clay
- Spools of thread
- Pencil
- Toothpick
- Scissors or craft knife
- Craft paint

Step 1
Roll several balls of clay in assorted sizes. Make imprints into the clay using the end of your thread spools. Use different-sized spools to make different-sized coin molds.

Step 2
Using a toothpick, edge the circular imprint with a row of pencil-point indents. Make designs for your coins, or write letters from the futhark (see page 28). Since this is a mold, the letters have to be written backwards. Allow the clay to dry.

Step 3
When your mold is dry and hard, press small balls of clay into the center of the coin mold. Make a fortune of coins by reusing the molds many times.

Step 4
Remove coins from the mold by pulling on the excess clay that spreads over the mold's sides.

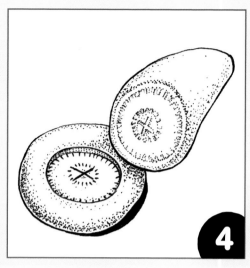

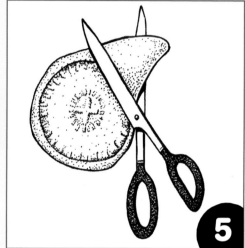

Step 5
Cut the excess edge with a knife or scissors, and smooth with your fingers.

Step 6
Once all the clay coins have dried, paint them with silver and gold paint. When dry, apply a coat of black paint and wipe it off with a paper towel. The black paint will enhance your etched details, making them look more authentic.

Decorative Arts

The Vikings were very fond of intricately crafted jewelry. By the ninth century, Viking metalsmiths were skilled in creating elaborate designs in silver, bronze, pewter, and gold-coated pieces, known as gilt. Jewelry, especially items crafted in silver, was sometimes covered in niello, a black, enamel-like substance that enhanced the intricacy of the design. The demand for jewelry was very high, and metalsmiths were kept busy creating brooches, bracelets, necklaces, and rings for arms and fingers. The demand for jewelry was so great that many religious artifacts that had been looted from monasteries were melted down and fashioned into new pieces of jewelry.

Wearing jewelry was a sign of wealth for the Vikings. Warriors were offered lavish gifts of jewelry from

Above are Thor's hammer pendants and the molds used to create them.

kings in appreciation of their fighting ability. Those who could not afford metal jewelry often created decorative pieces from the bones of animals.

Jewelry style was consistent throughout the Viking era. It was used to showcase many of the symbols that Vikings considered important, such as animal shapes with long, twisted bodies, or, much later, Christian crosses. One of the most popular religious symbols was drawn from Viking mythology: Thor's hammer. The hammer shape was thought to protect the bearer from hardship, or even death. The symbol was so common that there were molds made in order to produce it in mass quantities. Chains with pendants depicting Thor's hammer were commonly worn by Vikings even after the coming of Christianity, when they would be worn together with crosses.

The snake, which was thought to bring good luck, was another common symbol. The snake was an important character in many Viking stories, so it is not surprising that it is celebrated in the decorative arts. Writhing snakes may be found on everything from necklaces and bracelets to charms, amulets, and pendants. Other Viking motifs include dragons, cats, reptiles, and fish.

The Vikings also liked glass beads. Although glass was used much later in the Viking civilization and was usually imported from places like Germany and Russia, it became one of the most sought-after materials to use in creating their intricate and beautiful decorative arts.

The Vikings, believing that snakes brought good luck, decorated many items with them, including necklaces, bracelets, and pendants.

Thor's hammer was a popular religious symbol and was often worn as a pendant, like Christian crosses were worn in later eras.

Viking Jewelry*

Summon the power of Thor by making his famous hammer pendant, commonly worn by many Vikings.

* ADULT SUPERVISION IS REQUIRED FOR THIS CRAFT.

YOU WILL NEED
- **Salt clay (see recipe below)**
- **String**
- **Toothpicks**
- **Pencil**
- **Craft paint**
- **Salt**
- **Cornstarch**

Salt Clay Recipe
2 cups salt
1 cup cornstarch
1 cup water

Mix ingredients in a medium-sized saucepan. Heat over a low flame for approximately five minutes; stirring constantly. Remove from heat once it thickens. Allow clay to cool for ten minutes before kneading.

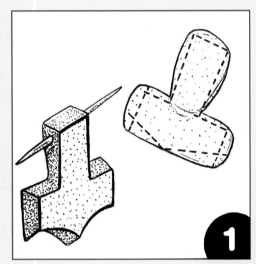

THOR'S HAMMER

Step 1
To make a Thor's hammer pendant, roll two small lumps of salt clay into tubes. Join them to form a T shape. Lightly flatten the tubes and cut straight edges with a butter knife. Take a toothpick and push it through the bottom of the T shape. This hole is where your string chain will pass through, so make it large enough for your type of string.

Step 2
Add details to your hammer pendant using a toothpick. Set aside to harden and make another piece of Viking jewelry.

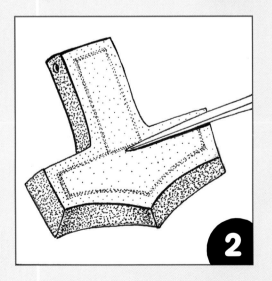

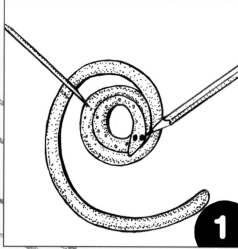

SNAKE CHARM

Step 1

To make a snake charm, roll a lump of salt clay into a long, slender tube approximately 14 inches long. Coil it into a spiral as shown, pinching the inside end into a point to make the snake's head. Decorate the body by making imprints with your pencil point.

Step 2

Roll a smaller lump of clay into a slender tube and attach it to the back of the snake, forming a loop. Allow the snake charm to dry and harden.

Step 3

To make chains for your jewelry, take three pieces of string, approximately the length of your arm, and tightly braid them. Paint your charms and the string with silver paint. When the silver dries, rub a small amount of black paint, using a paper towel, onto the surface of your charm and pendant. The Vikings used a black enamel called niello to highlight the designs of their jewelry in a similar way.

A New Religion

One of the most recognizable symbols of the Viking Age is the Jelling Stone, a monumental grave marker that was built by King Harald Bluetooth sometime between AD 965 and 985. The monument, which still stands today on the same site upon which it was erected in Jutland, Denmark, once marked the graves of Bluetooth's parents, King Gorm and Queen Thyre. The design of the monument is significant in that it marks the first use of Christian imagery in Scandinavia. One side of the three-sided stone is carved with the image of a great lion-like beast, and as is typical of traditional Viking design, its limbs are entwined like the coils of a snake.

Another side of the Jelling Stone is carved with an image of Christ, complete with outstretched arms and a halo. Archeologists believe that this image is the oldest of its kind in all of Scandinavia, and it has helped historians date the arrival of Christianity in the Viking lands. Long before the

This engraving features Harald Bluetooth, king of Norway and Denmark. The Viking leader converted to Christianity in AD 960.

majority of Vikings abandoned paganism, many absorbed Christianity into their culture to ease trade relationships between themselves and Christian lands. In some areas, it was even considered part of Viking law to embrace Christianity. Viking leaders often built monuments to commemorate those who fought bravely in battles, or to serve as a reminder of grand achievements. The majority of them were gravestones inscribed in elaborate interlocking designs and runes, which illustrated Viking sagas.

According to tradition, King Bluetooth converted to Christianity soon after witnessing a miracle that was performed by a Christian monk named Poppo. However, there is also speculation that he may have switched his faith for political reasons. The Jelling Stone is a tribute to King Bluetooth's parents, a testament to his conversion, and a commemoration of his reign. The monument, inscribed in runes, actually reads, "King Harald commanded this memorial to be made in the memory of Gorm, his father, and in memory of Thyre, his mother—that Harald, who won the whole of Denmark for himself and made the Danes Christian." Whether for political or spiritual reasons, Harald's conversion to Christianity ushered in a new era of Viking culture that was influenced by the traditions of the new faith.

Viking burial mounds were often arranged in the shape of a longboat, like the stones in the foreground.

The Jelling Stone (right) *is a monumental grave marker for King Harald Bluetooth's parents. It features the earliest image of Christ found in Scandinavia.*

The Jelling Stone*

Create a reproduction of the famous Viking Jelling Stone erected in Jutland, Denmark, by King Harald Bluetooth between AD 965 and 985.

* ADULT SUPERVISION IS REQUIRED FOR THIS CRAFT.

YOU WILL NEED
- **Sand clay (see recipe below)**
- **A pencil and paper**
- **Scissors**
- **Toothpicks**
- **Cardboard**
- **Watercolor paint**

Sand Clay Recipe
3 cups sand (beach or play sand)
1 1/2 cups cornstarch
3 teaspoons of powdered alum
2 1/2 cups of hot tap water

Combine all dry ingredients in a saucepan. Add the water and cook over a low heat setting. Mix continuously until thick and rubberlike. This should take roughly five minutes or less. Remove from heat. Pour the mixture onto your cardboard work surface. Allow it to cool for several minutes until it is warm to the touch. Begin kneading.

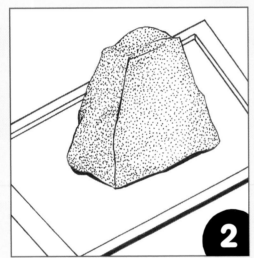

Step 1
Cut a piece of paper, approximately 5 inches by 7 inches, and draw a picture of your design. You can use the design on page 39 as a model. Cut out the design along each outside line with your scissors and set it aside. This is your stencil.

Step 2
Make the sand clay following the recipe shown above. Once the clay is cool enough, shape the mound into a large three-sided pyramid. Flatten the front side with your hand, making an even surface.

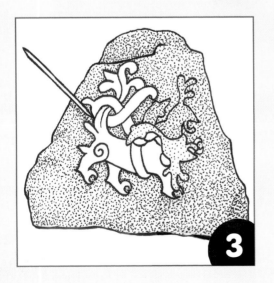

Step 3
Lightly press your paper stencil onto the surface of the wet clay. Trace its outline by cutting into the clay with a toothpick. When you are finished, peel away the stencil.

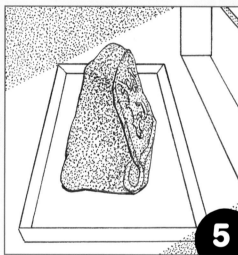

Step 4
Use the stencil as a guide to fill in the inside lines of your design. Draw designs of your choice around your central picture.

Step 5
When you are finished with your sculpture, place it in a sunny window to dry for two to three days. After the third day, lay the "stone" on its side, so the bottom can also dry.

Step 6
When your "Jelling Stone" is completely dry, give it a hint of color with watercolors.

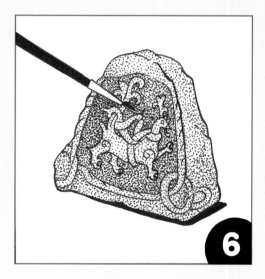

39

Leisure and Play

Despite the long hours it must have taken Vikings to provide for shelter, clothing, and food, they still found time for leisure activities. Men, women, and children played various sports and games, engaged in story-telling, and enjoyed music played on primitive instruments such as flutes, stringed harps, and lyres. These activities took place at Viking feasts, although musical entertainment mainly occurred in the more wealthy Viking households. Singing was also a popular pastime.

Feasts were extraordinary events during which everyone gathered to celebrate important seasonal holidays. At the feasts, there was a lot of food, drink, conversation, and joyful music. Tales of the Viking gods were told, poetry was recited, and jesters and jugglers danced, told riddles, and performed tricks for everyone's amusement. Historians believe that the Vikings also entertained themselves by watching fighting matches between horses and ponies.

Before sagas were written down, they were sung aloud to the music of harps.

During leisure time, Vikings engaged in activities such as swimming, wrestling, and a ball-and-bat game called *kingy*. Children often spent long hours playing with dolls and small wooden toys, or learning how to make decorative edges for clothing—a technique called tablet weaving. Young boys would often mimic their older brothers by playing with wooden swords. One of the most popular activities of all was playing board games.

Archeologists believe that some of the first board games ever built were crafted by Viking settlers, possibly to help them pass the time during the long, cold Scandinavian winters. They even believe that people may have played games similar to chess, with game pieces made from materials such as animal bone, amber, or glass. The Vikings called these games *hnefatafl*. Another popular board game, *merils*, was played by children and was very similar to checkers.

The most famous ancient game board was discovered in the city of Ballinderry, Ireland, which was once occupied by the Vikings. Believed to be based on an ancient Scandinavian game called Fox and Geese, this game board dates from the tenth century. The object of the Irish version of the game (called Brandub, or Black Raven, the traditional image of war) was to protect one's king against eight enemy pieces with the help of four knights.

These game pieces were used to play a Viking board game similar to chess.

The Ballinderry board was discovered in Ireland.
It is thought to date from the tenth century and is related to the board games that Vikings brought with them when they invaded Ireland.

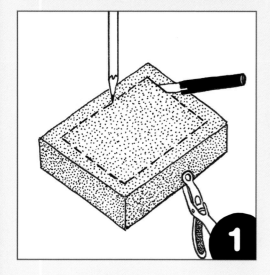

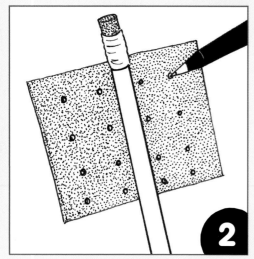

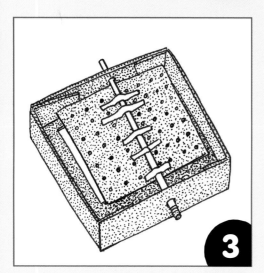

Viking Game Board*

Make a replica of the game board that was found in Ballinderry, Ireland. The Vikings probably used similar boards to play ancient games closely related to chess.

* ADULT SUPERVISION IS REQUIRED FOR THIS CRAFT.

YOU WILL NEED
- Cardboard box top
- Pencil, or dowel
- Air-drying clay
- Hole puncher
- Craft knife
- Ballpoint pen
- Craft paint
- Ruler
- Tape
- Glue
- String
- Toothpick

Step 1
Draw a 1/2-inch border around each side of your box top with a ruler to create the board's frame. Cut out the center with your knife and set aside. Punch a hole in the center of the front and rear side panels of the frame, approximately 1/2-inch from the bottom.

Step 2
Take the cardboard square you removed from the box top in step 1, and place your pencil (or wooden dowel) on the surface, as shown. Draw rows of tiny dots on the cardboard. Carefully puncture these dots with the tip of a ballpoint pen or pencil.

Step 3
Flip your frame over and insert the pencil (or dowel) through the holes of the frame as shown. Slip the cut piece of cardboard under the pencil and tape them together securely. The pencil should lie between the holes punctured in the cardboard.

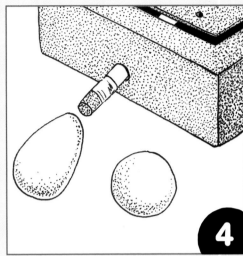

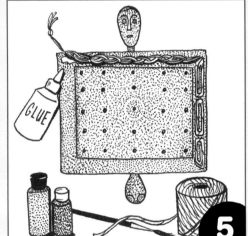

Step 4

Roll two lumps of clay into balls. Fit them onto the top and bottom of the pencil/dowel to create knobs. Allow the clay to dry. Using a toothpick, you can carve simple figures on these knobs, such as a king or serpent.

Step 5

Once the clay has dried, decorate the frame and knobs of the game board with glued pieces of string to give the illusion of detailed carvings. When the string dries, paint the game board with brown or gold paint.

Step 6

Make game pieces by taking very small lumps of clay and rolling them into balls. Pinch a tail into each ball. Each tail should be long and thin enough to fit into the board's holes. Make as many pieces as you desire and allow them to dry before painting. You can make your own rules for playing on the game board, perhaps using chess or checkers as a model.

TIMELINE

BC	**3500**	Egyptians develop first hieroglyphs.
	3200	Druids build Stonehenge.
	1333	Tutankhamun rules over Egypt and brings back the worship of many gods.
	1320	First papyrus book is made.
	776	First Olympic Games in Greece.
	500	Beginning of the Mayan civilization; Classical Age in Greece begins.
	336	Alexander the Great rules Greece.
	49	Julius Caesar rules Rome.
AD	**5**	Approximate birth of Jesus in Bethlehem.
	54	Nero becomes Rome's emperor and outlaws Christianity.
	117	Roman Empire is at its greatest point.
	138	Plague, war, and famine create unrest in Roman cities.
	286	Roman Empire is divided.
	312	Emperor Constantine rules and stops the persecution of Christians.
	330	Constantine makes Constantinople the capital of the Roman Empire.
	410	Roman Empire is reduced by barbarian attacks.
	793	Vikings begin attacking England.
	885	Viking siege of Paris, France.
	922	Viking discovery of Vinland (North America).
	958	Viking Harald Bluetooth becomes king.
	985	Viking discovery of Greenland.
	1200	Aztecs arrive in Mexico.
	1337	Hundred Years War between England and France.
	1341	Plague epidemic begins across Asia and Europe.
	1440	Beginning of the reign of Montezuma I, the greatest Aztec ruler.
	1450	Beginning of the Renaissance (rebirth of art and learning) in Europe.

GLOSSARY

althing   Yearly assembly of Vikings to discuss Viking law and settle disputes.

archeologist   One who studies civilizations by analyzing their artifacts.

artifact   Object, especially a tool, made by human craftsmanship.

berserker   Fierce Viking warrior of great strength and courage.

Birka   Highly populated merchant town in Sweden where Vikings would come to buy and sell goods; a trading village.

byrnie   Shirt made of tiny iron rings.

chainmail   Armor worn by wealthy Vikings; it is crafted of tiny, interconnected iron rings.

danegeld   Money and goods that were demanded by the Vikings in order to remain peaceful and nonviolent.

hnefatafl   Traditional Viking board game and pieces played like chess.

jarl   Powerful and wealthy Viking who owned land.

karl   Viking considered free by society; a merchant, craftsman, or farmer.

keel   Main section of a longboat that forms its narrow bottom edge.

kingy   Bat-and-ball game commonly played by Viking children.

longhouse   Viking farmhouse, so called because of its length.

lyre   Stringed instrument played during ancient times, especially to accompany storytelling and poetry.

niello   Black, enamel-like substance that metalsmiths rubbed over silver jewelry to enhance its design.

pagan   Person who worships many gods; a non-Christian.

pyre   Fire for burning a corpse during a funeral rite.

rune   Character (letter) in the Old Norse language.

saga   Story, often in the form of a poem, that tells of an expedition or a battle.

skald   Court writer, poet.

tapestry   Picture or design stitched or woven onto cloth that illustrates a story, an idea, or an event.

thatch   Natural material such as grass, reeds, or straw bunched together and bound to form the roof of a longhouse.

thing   Viking council that governed a community or group.

thralls   Viking slaves or prisoners.

Valhalla   Final home and resting place of Viking heroes slain in battle.

Vinland   The Viking name for North America when they discovered it.

ORGANIZATIONS

The Archaeological Institute of America
Boston University
656 Beacon Street, 4th Floor
Boston, MA 02215-2006
(617) 353-9361
Web site: http://www.archaeological.org

The University of Pennsylvania
    Museum of Archaeology
    and Anthropology
33rd and Spruce Streets
Philadelphia, PA 19104
(215) 898-4001
Web site: http://www.upenn.edu/museum

World Archaeological Society
120 Lakewood Drive
Hollister, MO 65672
(417) 334-2377
Web site: http://www.library.wustl.edu/units/
spec/archives/aslaa/directory/world-arch.html

In Canada

Ontario Archaeological Society
11099 Bathurst Street
Richmond Hill, ON L4C 0N2
http://www.ontarioarchaeology.on.ca

Royal Ontario Museum
100 Queen's Park
Toronto, ON M5S 2C6
Web site: http://www.rom.on.ca

WEB SITES

Dig! The Archaeology Magazine for Kids
http://www.digonsite.com

The Viking Resource Web
http://www.intercollege.se/viking

The World of the Vikings
http://www.pastforward.co.uk/vikings

FOR FURTHER READING

Gallagher, Jim. *The Viking Explorers*. New
    York: Chelsea House Publishing, 2000.
Martell, Hazel Mary. *Myths and Civilization
    of the Vikings*. New York: Peter Bedrick
    Books, 1998.
Sawyer, P.H. *The Oxford Illustrated History of
    the Vikings*. New York: Oxford University
    Press, 2000.
Steele, Philip. *Find Out About the Vikings*.
    London, UK: Southwater Publishing, 2000.
Time Life Books. *When Longships Sailed:
    Vikings, AD 800–1100*. New York:
    Time Life, 1998.

INDEX

ABOUT THE AUTHOR AND ILLUSTRATOR

Joann Jovinelly and Jason Netelkos have been working together on one project or another for more than a decade. This is their first collaborative series for young readers. They live in New York City.

CREDITS

SERIES DESIGN AND LAYOUT

Evelyn Horovicz